# Millie and her Mindful of mess

healthymindz.com.au

I dedicate this book to my bambinos;
my joy, my world, my inspiration.
Beck

nyskape.com.au

For my M's,
I hope I have inspired you to create,
and always chase adventure.
Morgan

Big learnings for growing minds.  First Edition. Printed 2020.

## YOUR WONDERFUL BREATH

*Your breath is the very first thing that enters you as you come into this world and the very last to leave. It is your longest, most loyal and faithful friend. IT IS THE CONNECTION TO LIFE.. In every moment your wonderful breath moves through your bodies unaided, unnoticed and unappreciated. You take between 17,000-24,000 breaths per day.... How many of these are you aware of??*

*Throughout this book I will ask you to STOP and breathe several times. This is to help you slow down, connect to your breath and to yourself. When you breathe with awareness It calms your nervous system, relaxes your body & mind, settles your emotions, connects you to your body and helps improve sleep.*

*Your breath is the doorway to your inner self. When you connect fully to each breath you are able to drop out of your busy minds and down into your inner being. It is here where you find peace and stillness. The breath is the KEY to all teachings to finding inner peace - Meditation, Mindfulness, Yoga and Tai Chi.*

*We need to teach our children the importance of the breath and its amazing abilities. For it will be with them every day, in every place, in every moment, ready to support them and take care of them. We as adults have held our breaths for too long, suppressing our emotions and losing our connection to our true selves. Please help your children learn a different way to be: self aware, connected, calm, confident, to be able to manage stress & emotions and most importantly be able to take care of themselves.*

*The quality of your breath is the quality of your life. Because without the breath we simply would not survive.*

# Millie and her Mindful of mess

"Hi, my name is Millie and this is Jasper my cat.

He is the greatest cat in the world!


When I grow up I want to be a vet, an astronaut or a zoo keeper.

I have a lovely mummy, a funny daddy and a crazy brother!

I love riding my bike, painting, swimming and having fun with my friends

but mostly spending time with Jasper."

As I begin to get ready for school, my mind starts thinking about EVERYTHING.

"Oh no, my mind is getting in a mess Jasper" I say to my furry friend.

I begin thinking about what was happening the other day and what might happen

later at school. Round and round all the thoughts go, messy and jumbled....

thoughts flying around, thinking about the past and the future....

and I just can't stop them...

...It feels like there are hundreds of bees and butterflies flying my thoughts around inside of my head, busy and buzzing.

"What's going on inside of my head? I can't stop thinking?

It's all gone crazy and I can't slow it down Jasper" I'm feeling so worried.

It then feels like some of the butterflies escape down into my tummy, fluttering and flipping inside of my tummy, the feelings are building stronger and stronger, and I'm feeling overwhelmed and I start to get angry.

I know this is when my body is telling me 'something's not right'.

Then I notice I'm feeling hot, my heart is beating really fast,

my hands feel sweaty and I feel like I'm going to explode....

I kick my backpack in anger and then I burst into tears.

"I've got my mind in a mess again Jasper" I cry angrily.

Jasper jumps on my lap to comfort me. He takes a big breath as he looks into my eyes.

"Oh yes, now I remember, I'm supposed to breathe" I sigh. "Thank you Jasper,

you helped me remember to deep breathe."

Three BIG, long, slow DEEP breaths, I Imagine I am blowing a feather along.

As I continue to focus on my breathing I begin to feel my mind slow down, I feel

my tummy calms as the butterflies settle and my whole body slowly relaxes.

This is when I come back into the present moment, the here and now.

I keep breathing slowly until I feel all the emotions have settled down inside of

me and I feel calmer. "That's better" I smile at Jasper "thank you for reminding me

and helping me, you're the best cat."

Now how did all this begin??????

Let me introduce you to Monkey Mind and Gentle Turtle.

These are the parts of me that I can hear, feel and connect to inside of me.

Monkey Mind is the trickster.

It wants you to believe all of its Monkey tales

and it doesn't always tell the truth.

Monkey wants to be the stronger and louder one.

When you focus on Monkey Mind it gains power.

It stirs up all the bees and butterflies and causes all the mess in the mind.

Monkey will tell you ANYTHING to get its power.

I usually find Monkey up in my head creating unhelpful thoughts, thinking about the past

(what has already happened) or the future (what might happen), making me

feel worried and telling silly stories that aren't always true.

Can you recognise any of these Monkey Mind thoughts inside of you?...

Nobody likes you

You're rubbish at this

This is all your fault

You can't do that

You're not good enough

No one understands

It always goes wrong

Take a moment to STOP. Take a breath.
What Monkey Mind thoughts or stories can you hear
inside of yourself today?
Remember, they're not always true.

Now, Gentle Turtle feels like my friend because it's a warm, kind feeling.

Turtle is always there to tell me the truth and I trust Turtle.

Gentle Turtle wants me to feel calm, relaxed and happy – in the here and now.

When I'm in this very moment I feel peace, I feel calm and I feel safe.

I usually find Turtle resting in my heart.

When I'm in this safe place I am able to hear Turtle's gentle, calm and loving words.

I hear all the great things about myself, wonderful, kind, inspirational, strong and positive.

It feels so good!! I feel peaceful and still.

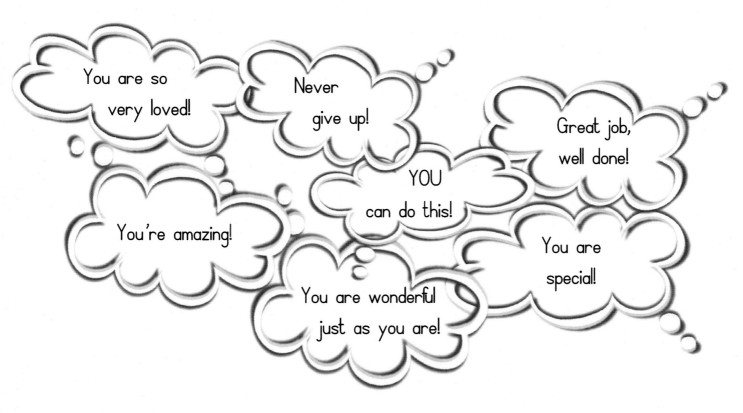

Now STOP and take 3 deep breaths.

Can you connect to Gentle Turtle inside of you?

What wonderful things can you hear or feel today?

14.

It's not always easy to hear Turtle. Turtle is gentle, soft and quiet,

whereas Monkey is very noisy and loud.

This is why it's SO important to STOP, BREATHE AND SLOW DOWN.

It allows the space and peace to hear what Turtle is saying.

This is where we hear our truth.

As I breathe I can feel myself dropping out of Monkey Mind, dropping down, down, down into my heart. "Oh Jasper, that's better. I feel much calmer and happier again. That Monkey Mind can really get me upset."

"Now now Jasper, there's no point in getting angry at Monkey. Monkey will always be with us. I have to learn to quieten Monkey as much as possible and be able to focus on feeling and connecting to Turtle instead."

16.

# TOP SECRET!

The secret I have found is to practise visiting this peaceful place inside of you everyday,

even if it's only for a few minutes.

The more you can connect to the Turtle down in your body,

the easier it becomes to breathe and calm yourself.


Just like everything, the more you practise the easier it gets, like riding a bike, reading,

spelling, times tables and writing. Everything gets easier the more you practise, including this.

As I continue to get ready for school, I talk to Jasper to ask him to help me
practise the ways that calm my busy Monkey Mind and help me connect to Turtle.

I put a teddy on my tummy and practise breathing deep and slow.

My tummy moves the teddy - up as I inhale and down as I exhale.

Sometimes I just imagine Turtle is riding my tummy as if on the ocean

bobbing up and down as it floats on the water,

relaxed and calm.

Another way I can calm myself is to pretend my fingertips have dandelions on them or flames like candles and I blow them one by one.
I take a big tummy breath and slowly blow them, imagining them floating away or going out, counting 1 2 3 4 5 6... until I feel calmer.
I end with a different number each time!

OR

I gently trace my lips with my finger, imagining I've traced a kiss and I blow it to Jasper.
I ALWAYS feel much better when I've practised these calming techniques.
"I better keep getting ready for school" I whisper to Jasper.

On the way to school I have a tummy ache again and I can feel the Monkey Mind telling me silly stories as my mum is about to leave me. I feel it happening again and there's no Jasper to help me, but this time mum does.

"It's just Monkey Mind playing tricks" she says, "focus on breathing, slowly and calming. Think of one of the calming techniques you like. You can do this Millie" mum says as she kisses and hugs me goodbye.

I don't want her to go...I feel the butterflies beginning...

I breathe and tell myself, I can do this. I blow my finger dandelions, slowly imagining them floating away. I feel my tummy going up and down. I got 10 fingers today. Yes!! I did it!!! I didn't get my mind in a mess!!! I feel so proud of myself.

I rush home from school to tell Jasper all about my day and how well I did

at ignoring the Monkey in my mind and doing my breathing all by myself!

He gives me the biggest cuddle and purrs loudly. I know he is proud of me too!

We have our dinner then I do my homework.

I play with Jasper outside before we have to start to get ready for bed.

24.

As I lay in bed and my mum and dad say goodnight I can feel the butterflies in my tummy and the Monkey in my mind starting to tell stories again......
and I'm finding it REALLY HARD to go to sleep.

"I can't get to sleep Jasper, I'm feeling all worried and the Monkey is back in my mind stirring up all my thoughts again." Jasper sighs,
(he really doesn't like the Monkey Mind getting me all worried and in a tizz).

Telling someone always helps me feel better, sometimes it's Jasper,
this time I go and tell mum.

"Mummy my mind is getting in a mess again and I feel really worried" I tell her.
"Ok darling, what's making you feel so worried?" she asks as she hugs me.
I shut my eyes and ask myself, what am I worried about?
"I'm worried about my test tomorrow" I realise.

"Ok sweetheart, you will be fine after a good night's sleep. Can you remember what you need to do?" Mum asks as we walk back to bed together.

I get back into bed and Jasper snuggles into me. I take a breath "I need to breathe to get out of Monkey Mind" I tell mum. "Yes Millie, that's it. So which is your favourite way to relax yourself to sleep that you have practised before?" asks mum. I think about another time when I felt calm and relaxed in bed. "My Turtle on a wave breath" I remember. "Yes Millie, that's a great one! Do you need my help or do you want to try by yourself?" mum asks holding my hand. Jasper looks at me and I feel him say "you can do this!" "I'm going to try myself mum" I smile. "I'm SO very proud of you Millie, I know you can do this" she gives me a kiss and a huge hug. "Night night darling and enjoy the ride!" she smiles and gives Jasper a wink. Jasper smiles at me as he snuggles into me....

he knows this is the best!

The Turtle wave breath is when I imagine a wave flowing from my heart down to different parts of my body, sending relaxation as it flows over me.

As I breathe out the wave flows out from my heart down my body and as I breathe in the wave flows back up to my heart.

As I close my eyes I begin with my 3 long feather breaths, as if I am blowing a feather up into the air. Jasper snuggles into me curled up and cosy.

I feel my body relaxing as I imagine myself dropping down into my body to find Gentle Turtle. I find Turtle resting on a wave of relaxation inside my heart.

*TIPS FOR PARENTS.*
The next pages are for you to read calmly to your children,
encouraging deep breathing as they relax into sleep
and to enjoy the meditation yourself!

I take a breath and as I breathe out,

I imagine a wave flowing down the body to the toes with Turtle riding on it...

sending relaxation to the toes.

I breathe in and the wave rolls back up, with Turtle enjoying the ride.

I breathe out, the wave flows to the feet,

feet are relaxed, the wave rolls back up.

I breathe the wave down to the lower legs,

calves are relaxed, the wave rolls back up.

I breathe the wave down to the knees, knees relax,

the wave surfs back up.

I breathe the wave down to the upper legs, thighs are relaxed,

the wave flows back up to the heart.

The whole legs feel heavy and relaxed.

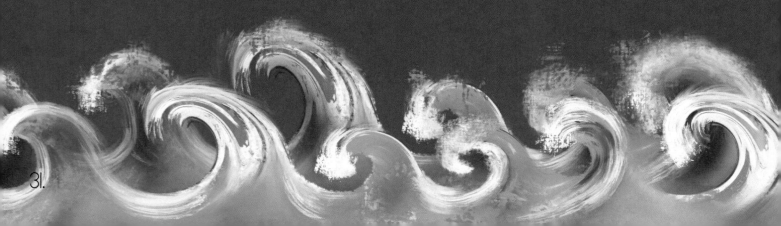

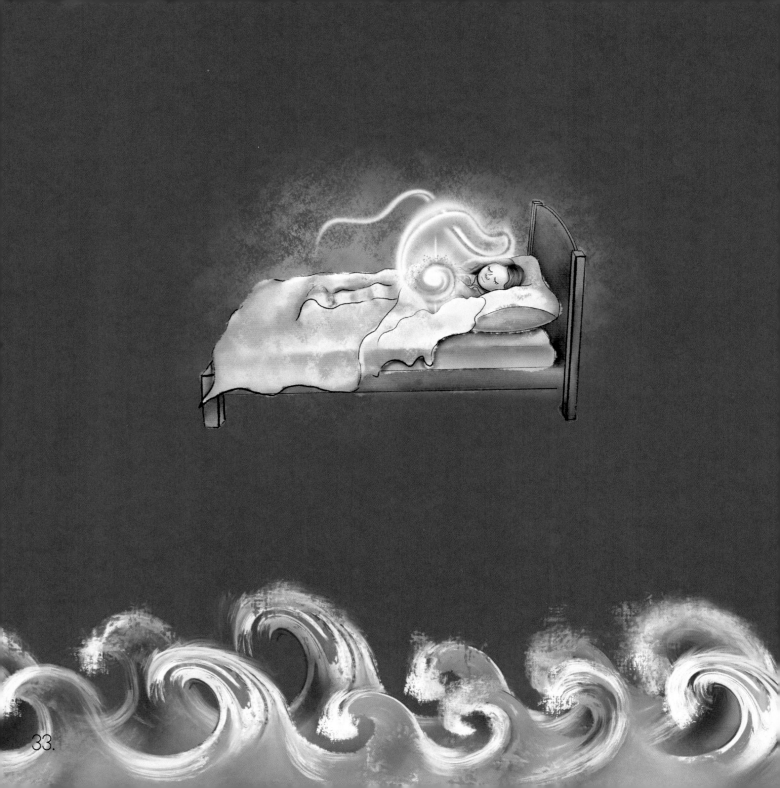

I breathe the wave down to the hips,

the whole lower body is relaxed, it feels floppy and heavy,

completely relaxed.

I breathe the wave into the tummy,

tummy feels soft and relaxed, the wave flows back to the heart.

I breathe relaxation into the whole chest,

chest expands like a balloon and relaxes back down.

I breathe into the whole back, it feels warm, soft and relaxed.

I breathe into the shoulders, they relax down feeling heavy and soft.

I breathe down both arms, they feel floppy, relaxed and heavy.

I squeeze the hands and I let go, letting my hands completely relax.

37.

I breathe up into the neck and ask it gently to relax.

I breathe as the wave flows over the face, sending relaxation to the whole face.

The jaw relaxes, the cheeks relax and the eyes drop back into cool pools of water.

The wave flows over the head, calming and soothing the head and the brain.

The wave flows over the whole body, from the head down to the toes.

The whole body is completely relaxed.

The wave flows peacefully from the tips of the toes to the top of the head,

heavy calm and peaceful.

Up and down the wave

flows, calmly, slowly until I am deep into sleep.

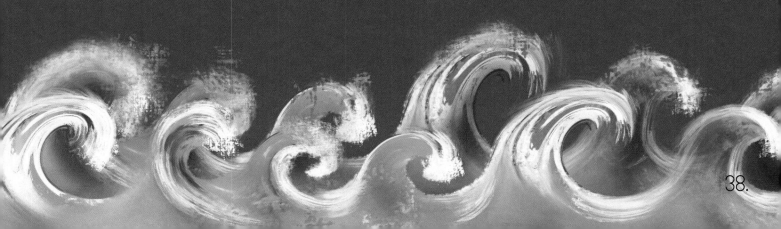

I wake up as I see the sun peeking through my curtains.

Oh yes the last thing I remember was my whole body was completely relaxed.

"We fell fast asleep, it was so lovely" I say to Jasper who's looking up at me.


"I DID IT!!! I DID IT ALL BY MYSELF JASPER!!! I CAN DO THIS, I CAN LISTEN TO

MY TURTLE INSIDE and keep my thoughts and feelings from becoming too big!".


I know Monkey Mind is still there wanting me to think about everything, especially

the past and the future but I feel Turtle so much easier now, as I've practised it so much,

the stillness and peace, in the present moment....


And I CAN stop my mind from getting in a mess!!!!

*Parents Information.*

Mindfulness is an ongoing practise for us all. The more we work this muscle (the brain), the stronger the receptors become and the muscle has memory therefore the more you practise the easier it becomes. Just like working any other muscle as it becomes stronger it gets easier. The best way to teach our children ANYTHING is to do it ourselves. As we know more is learnt through observation and learnt behaviours.

A great technique to help you is the acronym S T O P......
As soon as you can feel yourself beginning to react to a thought or feeling...

S...     Silence... remove yourself from where/who/what is triggering you,
          away to a quiet place (sometimes even the toilet!)
T...     Take 3-10 deep breaths.
O...     Observe your body, notice/watch where you might be feeling your reaction inside yourself and observe,
          not labelling it good or bad... it just is.
P...     Pitter Patter your feet on the ground...this will help ground you and might even make you smile,
          so you can go back to the world with a different perspective.

As you practise this more and more you will notice how much quicker you get at observing the rise of emotions or thoughts and not entering into them as you develop a deeper self-awareness. Catching those moments of stillness is the key.

On Pages 19 - 22 are techniques you can use to help teach your children calming and relaxation strategies when they begin to get overwhelmed with thoughts or emotions.

On Pages 31 - 38 is a relaxation meditation to teach your children how to calm and relax their bodies and minds. Each time this is practised the more natural it will become. The body recognises the effects and goes in to relaxation, deeper and easier. You might even find yourself in a relaxed meditative state too!!!!

May you all find your own Turtle peace, stillness and calm within. I hope my book can help you recognise your own thoughts and help them become quieter and tame the Monkey Mind. As you develop these skills and learn to observe your emotions, the art of Mindfulness will become a new way of life for you and your family.

Enjoy the amazing gift you have - YOUR FAMILY AND THE PRESENT MOMENT.


With Love,
Namaste

Made in the USA
Monee, IL
08 February 2022

90826946R00029